Catching My Soul

GEMORE BROWN

authorHOUSE®

AuthorHouse™
1663 Liberty Drive
Bloomington, IN 47403
www.authorhouse.com
Phone: 1 (800) 839-8640

Published by AuthorHouse 10/06/2015

ISBN: 978-1-5049-5538-6 (sc)
ISBN: 978-1-5049-5527-0 (e)

Print information available on the last page.

Any people depicted in stock imagery provided by Thinkstock are models,
and such images are being used for illustrative purposes only.
Certain stock imagery © Thinkstock.

This book is printed on acid-free paper.

Because of the dynamic nature of the Internet, any web addresses or links contained in
this book may have changed since publication and may no longer be valid. The views
expressed in this work are solely those of the author and do not necessarily reflect the
views of the publisher, and the publisher hereby disclaims any responsibility for them.

Contents

Among

I 'am fond

In your presence

Since

We met you

I knew

Where met to be

You and me

Falling in love

Of different feeling

For you

We do go through

Things

That chance

Us in the inside

Were each other guild

Can't hide

From your touch

We have a plane

That we can be in our land

When were more than friends

Love is deep

I feel it through my feet

Make me weak

You're in my heart

Can't be apart

Are you my mate?

It's my fate

We take each other souls

Want to unfold

With you

I feel feeling that I knew

You made

My emotions can't faded

I think of you

Your who

Is true

Me and you

Our love continue

And it's deep

We leap

To meet each other

Lover

No suffer

Being your soul mate

You can take

Me in your arms

We can get throw

Storms

In the rain

We'll walk together

With no shame

A thing our love can bring

Hope I can write you a note

Of how I feel for you

Deep emotions go's throw

You can bring me out of sorrow

And we follow

Each other path

To crate our craft

Falling apart

But my heart

Is building

For healing

Rumble

I find my place

Can't wait

Fate

We'll see me through

In what I do

I change

But the same

Bliss

In this

I think of hope

And write a note

And I can coup

My spirit is full

To continue

And be true

Feel the air

Can bare

To get through the struggle

A level

Can be too high

But can't deny

Lay

And wonder

I bubble of joy

That can't annoyer

Can change my mind

But shine

Carry me back

Don't fall flat

I path

That a have

Been

A sin

When

Sometimes

But I find my place

In my case

Feeling change what bring

Passion

Through my soul

Can't be cooled

I unfold

To my emotions

Struggle but luckily

Can be hope

That makes me coup

A flight

That can reach no height

I don't give up

Luck

Is in my corner

I feel I can ride obstacles

Levels

I can reach

A strive and won't stop

This what my feeling brought

Feelings are inside

If cried

Something dried

My tears

I build and heal

And feel

Still

I keep my emotions high

Were I can fly

Who would deny?

I see something in my path

That I have

I stumble

But humble

In a place of joy

That I can't annoy

I continue

To be how

I am no scam

Having feeling build

Heal

For tomorrow

Can be hollow

Inside

I glide

I confide

Knew what going through my soul

Throw

Nothing away

I piece together my feelings

Being

Aware

Things make heartache

But fate

Bring tears of joy

Can't give up

Luck

I can make it through

This I knew

Having you as my mate

I state

Is wonderful

You're my soul

We mold

Our love

Being with you

Make me build

And feel

My emotions

And you're my light

That I like no fright

Is love of bliss

Relationships

Won't ship

Fazes

Your love is bold

It unfolds

Will last

You're my heart

And you leave a mark

Hopping for change

Something can bring

Fame

Or walk in the rain

Holding my own

No wrong in my mind

I carry heavy emotions

But I confide

And don't hide

Feeling that I know

Of

I care with love

I care

Of what's there

In my heart

Struggle

But luckily

I pull

With full

Of emotions

I can't wait to see you face

I'll be surprise

That you arrive

To see

Me

We

Flee

To see

Each other

May we be together

Forever

This will be fine

You're me with me at any time

You who I confine in

When we meet

You keep

Attaching my heart

It might have been broken apart

I haven't felt this way before

We want more

We pore

Out are feeling

And telling

Our true emotions

Motion

To be at each other side

Make me high

Like I can glide

I feel deep emotions for you

What I'm going to do

With me and you

I feel that we can make it

Bit throw fits

Between is

You can crush my heart

Just the same when you can have it spark

A mark

But you find me in the dark

Love can be true

The loves want fade

What we made

Having you is good and bad

Have agreement

But we'll meant to be together

We'll get throw me and you

I knew that will be a true match

You catch

My heart

You is where I start

We struggle

But a couple

We are

My emotions fly high

With you don't have to be shy

Can't deny our passion

Our love is deep inside

We have a ride

Its fun

To love you

I hope you have love for me to

I struggle

At a level

That's out of reach

I keep

My emotions high

Inside

Follow my journey

Fully

With strength

That carries me through

I feel my sprit with thought

That brought joy

That I can't annoyer

I feel that I can fly

Can't be shy

As I lay

I think of a place

Were thing want chase

My thoughts

Something brought

Me hope

I coup

With my feeling

Something

In the distance

That follows me

Things crumble

But don't

Stumble

I hold my soul

As I stroll

I wish I could get close

You're the person I love the most

Love pores out for you

Who?

It's you

That has me high

Like I can fly

Your soul

I hold

In my heart

When we apart

I can't wait to see you

You do have an impact

Haven't been the same

Since we met

Think of you

And you're in my thoughts

You bring emotions

Take your potion

Fill under your

Spill

Its true love

Thinking of you

It get's deeper

Weather

It's good or bad

The emotions and feeling I had

Go's through my soul

Your love is bold

Can mold

My heart just for you

Deeper than friends

We've been

With each other

As lovers

We confine

Our love glide

Take our love further

As lovers

There no suffer'

Inside your near

Have no fear

Were here

Looking for love

Want somebody to have my heart

I look in the dark

Our soul can connect

I'll bet

Each other soul we'll hold

In place

In our case

Bliss

I wish

You'll be there

Where I am

I cram

Knowledge

Of you

This what I do

I deep passion

Catching us

I leap

To see you

Making me feel lovely emotions

It's deep

Feel it throw my toes

And feet

If feel weak

You strengthen my soul

You love takes it's told

I want to hold

And want the moment to last

You make a blast

In my spirit

I can feel it

Our love continue

Of bliss

If miss

Each other

We'll connect

And we're set

And I know you was the person for me

We speak of our feeling

Of the love

That of

And in our hearts

It thing

Are sorrow

We'll sing

You're my soul

And we unfold

Our love will last

Get don't go by fast

Want to hold the moment

We went with each other

Were lovers

No suffer

Time goes by

Still have healing that I can fly

You make me have wings

My soul sings

Hope your soul feels the same about me

Together

We

We tell our of different feeling

You're my match

You catch my heart

Something are wonderful

Full of life

Can be shaper than I knife

Thinking of hope

That can't be broken

I feel bliss

And I wish

This would last

What has

Happen

Life as me high

I lay

And wonder

If what we'll happen tomorrow

I follow

Something inside

We'll glide

You to a place

In your case

You'll find hope

You'll find

Your claim

Walls

With hope on your side

You're glide

To your dreams

Streams you can walk on

Fun in your heart

Nothing can make you fall apart

Trust

You must

Don't rush

Things bring you joy
in some sad emotions

Motions

To suecces

You can rest

Thing change

Strange

Feelings are inside

As we ride

Our love

In a space

When my heart race

For you

Wonder if you feel the same

You're my soul mate

What's in my heart

No person can reach me like you do

Thinking of you

This love feels s true

In what we do

Things in side burn

Earn

To walk a path

Ways
that have mazes

Fazes

What stop me

What can be?

Finally

I lead if weeds

Get to high

Can't deny

My impact

Try not to lack feeling

Thinking of a time

Were I clime

Walls

Sometime calls

In the air

Were

I walk

Reaching for balance

I continue my journey

Things burning inside

Inside

Don't let sorrow

Harm me

For tomorrow

Shallow

Images fill my mind

But shine

Hoping my plan want sake

In the sand

Were I been

Build me

Hold heartily

Thinking of you bring life out of sprit

I can feel it

When we meet

My soul leap

If I weep

You can dry

My eyes

I like when you lay

With me

Full of

Soul

That you hold

What you bring

No shame

Thinking of you

Have me high

In my arms you'll lay

Always bring me joy

That I can't annoyer

That the hold you have on me

We love each other

No suffer

You make me feel glade

With the feeling I had

About you

I hope you think of me to

You make me feel new

Inside

Their love of

Different

Emotions

You're in my heart

Were we start

We gather feeling

Telling

What in our heart

For each other

No suffer

When I see you

Passion

Catching

My heart in your soul

Things unfold

Can't cry

Your there

To prepare

And confide in each other

Were lovers

Our love will live

Is what we feel

Build

And shell

Can't wallow

Can wait to see you tomorrow

What will come next?

You can text

Me and tell me how you feel

You can revile

Your thoughts

And what brought

Joy that you can't

Annoyer

When you r with me

You make me feel full

Not empty

Finally

Fond somebody that can reach me

In my heart

Don't like it when where apart

You hold

And mold

My feelings

A sensitive spot that you have inside of me

You make me feel lovely

You're my soul

We unfold

Our feeling

And have healing

Wish you'll be there

Where

I am

By my side

Empty inside

If I can tell you how I feel

It's your love can shell and heal

You can have over my heart

Feel like I know you

And what you do

You have an impact on me

Thinking of you bring lovely feelings

Wonder how to get your attention

I mention

That I have feeling

That healing

For you

Hope you feel the same way to

Thinking you can be my mate

Is fate

For us to be a couple

Luckily

You fit

The person I want to be with

What inside of you

I hope you do

Tell me your thoughts

You're my life

You is

Who

I want to be with

You can heal

When things spill

Feel

Emotions

That can build

Can't shell

From your love

I think of you in my mind

And can't until it's time

For us to met

It's a sanative thing

How you make me sing

Wings you can make me fly

If I was shy

It went away

If they want to know

I tell them my feeling that go's

Throw

With me and you

You have my heart

Like a cart

Of bloom

Your soul is bright

Our love is out of sight

Wonder about you

And how you feel about me to

Were soul mates

That crates

In our soul

Can't go without you

You have a hold on me

Completely

You bring something out of me

Finally

I fond love

Thinking of you

Want to be with you

And we can do

Everything together

Any weather

You bring joy

That I can't annoyer

It comes out of my heart

And it leaves a mark

You're my hope

I write in this note

You're my soul

We unfold

Having you by my side

My soul glide

Confined

In you

What I do

It's true

The love we have

Me and you

Can make it throw

I wonder what we'll be next

Catch my soul in your heart

Can't be apart

You're the person I can count on

Is fun

To have a soul mate

We crate

Love

Of our feelings

It's healing

To have you at my side

We glide

In space

In case

You're not there

You're still my heart

If we grafted apart

You're my heart

In my mind

Some kind

Of spell

A shell

We can protect

For each other

Can't wait

If fate

That were a couple

You're still the person for me

We

Connected

Want let

Things destroy our love

Of

Different kinds of feelings

That we hold

It unfold

Our emotions

We've been there on each other side

That's what we strive

To do

Ma and you

Our love build

And we shell

Each other

From sorrow

You'll my tomorrow